Helping at the Library

Step by Ste

Dale Dixon

COMPUTER SCIENCE For the REAL World™

Rosen Classroom™

The library is a great part of my community. People come here to find books to read.

Reading is important. The librarian helps each person find a book.

How can I help at the library? The librarian says I can put books in order.

The librarian wants me to sort the books by subject. She says I can do it step by step.

The librarian hands me a list of subjects. The subjects are animals, space, countries, and crafts.

First, I look for books about animals. That's the first subject on the list. I find books about sharks, cats, and snakes.

“Next, look for books about space,” says the librarian. I find books about stars, moons, and planets.

Then, I look for books about other countries. I find books about India and Mexico.

Last, I find books about crafts. Some books teach readers how to sew. Some books teach readers how to paint.

The librarian says, “Thank you!” Sorting books at the library was fun. I learned how to sort them step by step!

Words to Know

librarian

library

sew